WILDLI
AUSTRALIA

Australia is home to some of the world's most remarkable animals. Many exist nowhere but on this island continent, with its unique landscapes.

Wildlife and landscapes, or animals and habitats, have been inextricably entwined for the fifty million years that Australia has been separated by ocean from the rest of the world. For long ages, it was a place of rainforests and lakes. During a slow drift northwards, the land became warmer and drier. The ancestors of today's animals and plants adapted or perished as vast inland lakes evaporated and rainforests shrank coastwards, to be replaced by eucalypts and acacias. Many creatures, such as the Koala, the marsupial gliders and birds known as honeyeaters, formed partnerships with these drought-resistant plants.

Humans arrived in Australia and kept on altering the landscape, reducing some habitats, encouraging others and creating some new ones. These changes have accelerated in the past 200 years: today some of Australia's animals, such as the larger kangaroos, are common and obvious, while others, such as the Numbat, are rare and difficult to observe.

The animals shown in this book are examples of creatures that live in the habitats described. They are not confined to these areas, and some species, such as the Common Brushtail Possum, are found in many environments. These versatile species have the best chances of long-term survival. For far too many Australian mammals, in particular, continued existence outside special reserves depends on the conservation of their natural habitat.

PASCAL
PRESS

The Koala makes its home in eucalypt trees. **Clockwise from above left:** A drowsy Koala wedges itself securely into a fork; a Koala's digestive system contains tiny organisms that break down the tough fibre in its diet of leaves; a Koala will eat the choicest leaves available; a relaxed Koala displays the long limbs and sharp claws that make it a skilful climber; clad in dense fur, a Koala lives in the branches and does not shelter in a nest or den; a young Koala surveys the world.

Above: *Eucalypt trees stand tall above a "marsupial lawn" cropped by kangaroos.*
Inset, left: *A pair of tiny Feathertail Gliders.* **Inset, right:** *A Crimson Rosella perches on the distinctive bark of a eucalypt tree.*

EUCALYPT FORESTS

About 700 species of eucalypt are found in Australia. Their hard, often waxy, leaves prevent precious water from evaporating when the weather is hot and dry, and most species are fire-resistant. Ranging from the mighty Mountain Ash that may grow 95 metres high to stunted desert mallees, eucalypts bear blossoms rich in nectar that attract all sorts of sweet-loving mammals, birds, bats and insects. These trees' hollowed trunks and branches provide homes for climbing and flying creatures, and their canopies shelter a whole complex of ground-growing plants and their wildlife tenants.

Strangest of the eucalypts' associates is the Koala, whose only home is the branches. This appealing marsupial eats only carefully chosen leaves and sleeps 19 hours out of every 24.

The coastal wet eucalypt forests of Australia's south-east and south-west have very tall, old trees that tower above dense understoreys of ferns and shrubs. Parrots, possums, gliders and owls live and nest in the hollows formed by time in these forest giants, while the ground has its own population of kangaroos, wallabies, bandicoots and birds, including the Superb Lyrebird. The drier forests further inland harbour their own fascinating animal residents, which once included the termite-eating Numbat, perhaps the most beautiful of marsupials. Today, the Numbat exists in only a few protected forest areas. When eucalypts blossom, they all are restaurants for honeyeaters and other nectar-eaters.

Top: A Squirrel Glider feeds on the nectar of eucalypt blossoms.   **Above, left:** The Sugar Glider can swoop between trees on furry membranes linking fore- and hind-limbs.   **Above, right:** The Yellow-footed Antechinus is a small insect-eater.

Above, left: *Portrait of a Grey Kangaroo.*   **Above, right:** *A female Grey Kangaroo with a large joey in her pouch.*
Below: *A Grey Kangaroo and her almost independent joey rest during the heat of the day. A much smaller joey may be attached to a nipple in the female's pouch.*

Above: *A young Tasmanian Devil lays claim to some of the meal being devoured by its mother. The largest living marsupial carnivore, the Devil may be a predator or a scavenger.*
Below: *The Numbat eats termites that it licks up with its long, sticky tongue. It is one of the few day-active marsupials and has become very rare because of predation by the fox.*

Above, left: *This female Red-tailed Black-Cockatoo eats eucalypt seeds, prising them from their hard gumnuts with its strong bill.*
Above, right: *The Laughing Kookaburra lives in a family group that greets the dawn with a rollicking territorial chorus.*
Below: *On a display mound scratched together on the forest floor, a male Superb Lyrebird sings and dances to attract a mate.*

Above: *The Mallee Fowl's sand nest is a huge incubator. The male Mallee Fowl tests the warmth of the sand each day, then adds or scrapes away material to keep the eggs within at a constant temperature.* **Below, left:** *An Australian Ringneck parrot perched in a tree.* **Below, right:** *The Short-beaked Echidna breaks into termite mounds with its powerful claws. The insects are detected with organs sensitive to electricity on the echidna's snout, then retrieved with its long, sticky tongue.*

MALLEE AND MULGA

Mallees are multi-trunked eucalypt trees that grow from a swollen central root. They dominate many of Australia's semi-arid landscapes, often with shrubs and clumps of grass scattered between them. "The Mallee", as this country is known, can have a rich wildlife population, but all too often mallee country has been cleared for wheat farming. The Mallee Fowl, a ground-dwelling bird that incubates its eggs in a huge mound of sand, is a notable occupant.

"The Mulga" is dry country in which the chief trees are species of acacias, or wattles. The roots of acacias harbour bacteria that help the trees to make the most of soil nutrients. Mulga wildlife can endure long periods of drought, and, after good rain, their homeland blossoms and briefly becomes a paradise of wildflowers, nesting birds and frantically reproducing insects, frogs and small mammals.

Above: *Mallee habitat is typified by multi-trunked eucalypt trees, hardy shrubs and sandy soil.*
Inset: *The Shingleback is a large skink. A female gives birth to two, or sometimes three, live young.*

Above: *Hummocks of spinifex surround Kata Tjuṯa, Uluṟu–Kata Tjuṯa National Park, Northern Territory.*
Inset: *The Spinifex Pigeon feeds on the seeds of spinifex grasses.*

SPINIFEX

Spinifexes are needle-leaved grasses that flourish in desert landscapes, their hummocks covering over 15 per cent of Australia. New growth rises on the outside of a spinifex hummock so that, as old growth dies, the mound gradually becomes a ring. During the day, the spinifex is home to birds and reptiles – hunting monitors, basking smaller lizards and the occasional snake. After dark, a whole new cast of characters enters, criss-crossing the red sand between hummocks. Hopping-mice skitter about, feeding on spinifex seeds, soft-skinned geckoes stalk small prey, while beetles and ants scuttle on foraging expeditions like tiny clockwork toys. If you could but hear it, the still air would carry a gentle murmur, the soft chomping of millions of tiny jaws, as the termites snip off lengths of spinifex to carry back for storage in the rock-hard mounds that rise like red fortresses among the gold-green spinifex.

Top, left: *Spinifex Hopping-mice do not need to drink, for they metabolise water from their seed diet.* **Top, right:** *The carnivorous Kowari lives in stony desert country, where it shelters in burrows during daylight.* **Above:** *A Sand Monitor tracks its prey through the spinifex, "tasting" the scent with a long, forked tongue.* **Below:** *One of the most beautiful of Australia's marsupials, the Bridled Nailtail Wallaby, was once common in spinifex country, but now survives only where protected from introduced predators.*

Above: *The Dingo, a predator at the top of the food chain, may hunt alone or form part of a family pack led by a breeding male and female.*

Below, left: *The Bilby is a silky-furred bandicoot that digs long burrows to hide in during the day. It feeds at night on insects and fungi.*

Below, right: *The Smooth Knob-tailed Gecko stalks smaller geckoes and insects across the dunes at night. Like all geckoes, it has fixed, transparent eyelids.*

SAND DUNES

The burning red hues of Australia's sandy deserts come from the fine layer of iron oxide enclosing each tiny grain of sand. The wind-blown dunes that are such vital features of these regions may be 200 metres high and a kilometre wide. Between them are depressions, or corridors, where water that collects after infrequent rain nurtures hardy plants. One of these dune complexes may be home to 40 species of lizard, all of which eat insects and other lizards. They, and the small mammals that burrow to escape the heat of the day, form prey for birds, snakes, monitors and Australia's wild dog, the Dingo.

A dawn walk amongst the dunes reveals to the human observer that the surface of the sand is cross-hatched with the intersecting tracks of nocturnal adventurers, overlaid by the toes-and-tailtips trails of birds, up early to snap up any small creature not safely home at first light.

Above: A sand dune in central Australia covered with short-lived blossom after a rare heavy shower of rain.
Inset: The Thorny Devil eats only small, black ants. It drinks dew that collects on its skin during the cooler night.

Above: *This gorge was cut through a sandstone range by a river that is now just a chain of pools.*
Inset: *The Wedge-tailed Eagle soars above desert ranges, watching below for unwary wallabies or other prey.*

INLAND RANGES

Lifted up by cataclysms of the earth more than 300 million years ago, Australia's inland ranges have been worn down by weather, water and time. However, like island chains in an ocean, some rise to a thousand metres above the continent's great central plateau and, also like islands, they provide sanctuary for a variety of animals. The great rivers that once carved ravines through their sandstones now exist only as underground soaks, and, in good seasons, tree-bordered waterholes. However, there are permanent pools in steep-sided gorges and occasional springs trickling from the rock.

Desert ranges are refuges for threatened species such as rock-wallabies. Cliffs, caves and overhangs provide shelter from the burning desert sun and refuge from predators, and are homes to bats, possums and pythons. Soaks, springs and waterholes attract creatures great and small, including frogs, finches, pigeons, parrots and wallaroos.

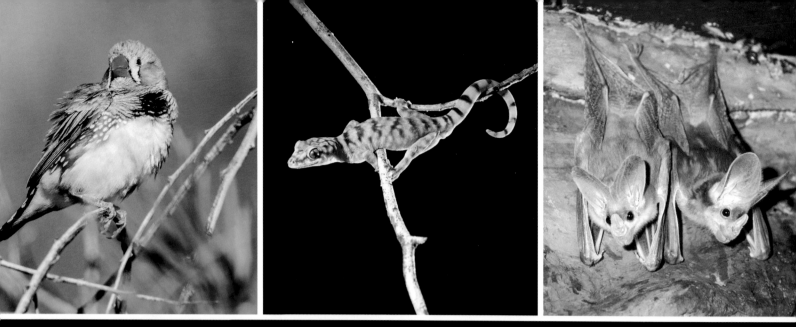

Above, left to right: *Zebra Finches feed on dry seed and often visit water to drink; the Giant Cave Gecko is found in sandstone ranges across northern Australia; the Ghost Bat lives in caves and mine shafts – it hunts small creatures, including other bats.* **Below, left:** *A Yellow-footed Rock-wallaby pauses in its flight up a rockface.* **Below, right:** *Black-footed Rock-wallabies breed all year round.* **Bottom, right:** *The Black Wallaroo lives on the steep Arnhem Land Escarpment.*

Above, left: *Blue-winged Kookaburras are found around wooded watercourses in northern Australia.*   **Above, right:** *A Sulphur-crested Cockatoo stretches after drinking.*
Below, left: *The Galah is a cockatoo that travels in large, screeching flocks. When Galahs visit water, they spend a lot of time interacting with other flock members.*
Below, right: *The Water Rat lives along the banks of rivers and around permanent waterholes, and is a good swimmer. It eats yabbies and other aquatic creatures.*

BILLABONGS AND INLAND RIVERS

Across the arid heart of Australia, rivers loop and wander, sometimes disappearing underground, sometimes lying in meanders bordered by long-rooted eucalypts. Cut-off bends called billabongs are surrounded by reeds and paperbark trees. After good rain, the watercourses roar into life, spreading out across their floodplains, only to shrink again under the rays of the outback sun.

In dry times, water is life to the creatures of the inland. Some come boldly to drink during the heat of the day, but most try to quench their thirst around dawn or in the late afternoon. Doves and pigeons dash to the shallows to suck up a drink and escape before they are taken by a bird of prey. Emus scoop up beakfuls, raising their heads to watch for danger as the water runs down their long throats. Cockatoos gather in huge, noisy flocks in waterfront trees, sparring and shrieking in an avian version of party time, cementing social bonds while they wait for the first brave soul to flap down to the water's edge and lure out of hiding any lurking bird of prey.

Above: *Eucalypts border the course of an inland river, providing homes, nest sites and refuges for diverse creatures.*
Inset: *A Brown Falcon sits in a tree by a billabong, watching alertly for stragglers from the flocks of doves coming to drink.*

Above: *The plains in a dry year.* **Inset, left:** *Budgerigars mating after rain has fallen on the grasslands.*
Inset, right: *A Major Mitchell's Cockatoo feeds amongst seeding grasses in a good season.*

THE PLAINS

The great grassy plains that cover so much of Australia's outback are prized for grazing cattle and
sheep. These seemingly limitless grasslands are home to the heraldic beasts of the Commonwealth of
Australia, the Red Kangaroo and the Emu. Both have benefited from the provision of watering points
for stock. A rarer sight is the Australian Bustard, a large, insect-eating bird that was hunted for the pot
by generations of pastoralists and travellers. Today, it is making a comeback and can be seen stalking
majestically between the tussocks. If pressed, it unfolds intricately-patterned wings to float away into
the heat-haze. In dry times the tussocks may be cropped to their roots and the country seems dead.
However, like so many inland areas, the grasslands flourish after good rain. Birds appear as if by magic
as the grasses sprout, mature, then seed. Parrots such as the Budgerigar breed wherever they can find
nest hollows, then form great flocks that fly in shimmering, ever-shifting formations of wonderful
colour and fill the air with the whirring of wings.

Above, left: *A Red Kangaroo hopping across the plains.* **Above, right:** *The Euro is a stocky kangaroo with thick, shaggy fur.*
Below: *A fully grown male Red Kangaroo (left) may weigh up to 85 kilograms. The strong fore-limbs are used in fighting with other males, or to grasp an attacker.*

Above, left: *Major Mitchell's Cockatoos flock to feed on the grasslands.*

Above, right: *The Australian Bustard stalks the plains looking for insects to eat. It appears in numbers when grasshopper plagues invade the grassland.*

Below: *Emus are large, flightless birds found across most of inland Australia. Male emus incubate the eggs and raise the chicks.*

Many large grassland creatures, such as kangaroos, emus and cockatoos, move to new pastures when an area is eaten out. They return after rain sprouts new green shoots. Smaller mammals, reptiles and frogs are not mobile enough to migrate when the plains dry up. They take refuge underground, in the cool depths of the cracks opened up in the sun-baked topsoil. Here they survive until rain falls again, transforming the flats first into shallow swamps and then into rippling seas of grass.

In northern Australia, scattered clumps of trees transform the plains into park-like tropical savannah. These trees offer feeding, nesting and refuge opportunities to a variety of birds and to reptiles such as the Frilled Lizard.

Top, left and right: *The Bearded Dragon and Fat-tailed Dunnart hunt insects amongst the grass tussocks.*
Above: *The Frilled Lizard is a savannah dweller. It opens its neck frill to bluff would-be attackers.*

Above: *Winter visits the forested high country of the southern Great Dividing Range.*
Inset: *The Corroboree Frog survives winter's freezing temperatures in the Australian Alps.*

COASTAL MOUNTAINS

Australia's major chain of mountains, the Great Dividing Range, runs down the continent's eastern seaboard, extending from Cape York Peninsula through Victoria (and as far west as the Grampians) to Tasmania in the south. The short rivers that flow down the steeper eastern slopes of the ranges to the Pacific Ocean pass through wet forests, while, to the west of the watershed, the country is much drier. The highest point of these mountains, the Australian Alps, contains Mt Kosciuszko (2228 metres); it has its own unique fauna, including the tiny Mountain Pygmy-possum, which sleeps winter away in a snug nest under the snow, and the brilliantly coloured Corroboree Frog, found only in beds of sphagnum moss. Along most of the southern part of the Great Divide, birds and larger mammals feed in the high country during summer, then move to the lower levels for winter. In the north this seasonal movement is less marked. On the coastal heights of these northern mountains, wet eucalypt forest gives way to rainforest, which is home to many strange and amazing creatures.

The forests and woodlands of the Great Divide are home to colourful parrots.
Clockwise from above left: *The Eastern Rosella flies in small family parties; the male Australian King-Parrot is at home in mountain forests or in gardens in cities and towns; his mate is less brilliant, but no less beautiful; Gang-gang Cockatoos move to the high country of south-eastern Australia in summer, and to lower altitudes during winter.*

The Platypus lives in unpolluted fresh water down the east coast of Australia, from alpine creeks to tropical rivers. Magnificently adapted to finding its food in water, it lays two eggs in a nest dug into the bank of a watercourse, then the babies that hatch from the eggs feed on their mother's milk.

The Common Wombat, a large but agile marsupial, forages for grass and tubers on mountain slopes, sheltering during the day in large burrows dug into sloping ground. Grey Kangaroos, Koalas, wallabies and gliders are also common in coastal mountains. Less obvious are the nocturnal, predatory quolls and various small kangaroo relatives such as potoroos and pademelons, whose numbers are all too often kept in check by the fox and other introduced hunters.

Top: *The Platypus hunts under water with its eyes shut, tracking prey by the tiny bursts of electricity its body gives off.*
Above, left: *The Spotted-tailed Quoll is the largest marsupial predator on mainland Australia. Males weigh 3–4 kilograms.*
Above, right: *The Long-nosed Potoroo needs dense cover for survival. It is common only in parts of Tasmania.*

Above: *The Common Wombat spends daytime in a large burrow, emerging to graze at dusk. Although wombats may share a burrow, they live solitary lives.*
Below: *Red-necked Wallabies are common in coastal forests in south-east Australia. In mountainous areas and in Tasmania they grow thick coats of shaggy fur in winter.*

Above, left: *The long finger on the paw of the Striped Possum is used to prise insect larvae from their hiding places.* **Above, right:** *A Common Spotted Cuscus pauses in its slow progress through the branches, eating leaves, fruit and insects.* **Below, left:** *The Herbert River Ringtail Possum lives in mountain rainforest in north Queensland.* **Below, right:** *The Green Ringtail Possum spends the day curled asleep on a broad branch. Its fur is grey, grizzled with silver, yellow and black to appear greenish.*

Above: *Tropical rainforest in Queensland's Wet Tropics World Heritage Area.*
Inset: *Lumholtz's Tree-kangaroo is found only in north-east Queensland's tropical mountain rainforest.*

RAINFORESTS

Fifty million years ago, rainforest spread over large areas of Australia. Today, these forests cover only about 0.3 per cent of the continent. Three-quarters has been destroyed since 1788, and the forest that remains is a national treasure. The animals of north Queensland's tropical rainforests have evolved in harmony with a botanist's paradise of plant life. The canopies of the towering trees attract fruit- and nectar-loving birds, bats and insects. Tree-trunks and vines, with their epiphytic orchids and ferns, are home to mammals, frogs and reptiles, while the forest floor harbours a wealth of small invertebrates, and more mammals, frogs and ground-loving birds. A rainforest may seem deserted. The observer should wait a while in silence, listening for the sounds that betray parrots or pigeons plundering fruit high above. Close examination of trunks and creepers is sure to reveal geckoes, moths, spiders and other creatures that escape notice because they blend with their surroundings.

When rainforest trees flower or fruit, they do so in abundance, attracting birds from far and wide to the feast. Lorikeets, with their brush-tipped tongues and brilliant plumage, jostle for dining space with sugar-loving honeyeaters. Pigeons, parrots and figbirds gulp down some fruits and dislodge others that fall to the forest floor only to be snapped up by horny-helmeted cassowaries and strutting brush-turkeys.

Bowerbirds swallow some of the bounty, but the males carry choice items to the avenues of twigs they build as display grounds. These fruits, flowers and other treasures of the correct colour are arranged and rearranged until a female visits the "bower". Then the male sings and mimics at his loudest, strutting and prancing, eyes bulging and plumage quivering, until the female either flies away or succumbs to his charm. He plays no part in nesting or bringing up the chicks.

Above: *A male Satin Bowerbird displays for the female attracted by his song to his avenue of sticks painted with plant juices and saliva. He will dance and show off the treasures he has gathered before mating with her in the bower.*

Above, left: *Rainbow Lorikeets perch on the rim of their nest hollow.* **Above, right:** *The flightless Southern Cassowary may measure two metres from its powerful feet to the top of its helmeted head.* **Below, left to right:** *Three birds of the forest canopy – a male Eclectus Parrot, a Rose-crowned Fruit-Dove and a female Eclectus Parrot.*

Clockwise from above: *The Orange-eyed Tree-frog lives in the forest canopy, descending to ground level after heavy rain to find pools of water in which to breed; the Green Tree Python hatches as a yellow baby and changes colour some time between two and three years of age; the Pig-nosed Turtle lives in northern streams; a Red-legged Pademelon shelters in the forest during the day.*

Many of the most fascinating creatures of the rainforest prefer to go through life unnoticed. They may, like some reptiles, frogs and insects, be exquisitely camouflaged so that a predator's eye will pass them unseeing. They may, like ground-dwelling pademelons and other small mammals, spend the daytime dozing, only rousing to hop quietly to open spaces and graze after dusk confuses shadow and substance. Night-time is playtime and mealtime for possums of many sorts, tree-kangaroos, owls, skin-winged blossom-bats and flying-foxes. Daytime sees rainforest clearings a-glitter with the iridescent wings of butterflies. Often the caterpillars from which these magnificent insects metamorphose have fed on poisonous leaves. The butterflies' brilliant coloration warns that the toxins from this infant diet linger in their bodies, and will discomfort predators foolish enough to eat them.

Above: *A pair of mating Cairns Birdwing Butterflies. The female is above, the male below.*
The caterpillars of this splendid butterfly feed on native Aristolochia *and* Pararistolochia *vines.*

COASTAL WETLANDS

Australia's wetlands may be permanent or temporary, natural or made by humans. The water they contain may be fresh, brackish or salty, still or flowing. They offer many sorts of habitats for animals and contain plants as different as pandanus palms, paperbarks, bottlebrushes, reeds and mangroves. Permanent wetlands have resident populations of fishes, frogs and lots of other aquatic creatures. Temporary swamps, which fill during the wet season and dry out again when the rains cease, are no less rich in animals, but harbour species such as birds that can fly away when the water evaporates, or frogs and turtles that disappear into the mud and sleep away the dry times to emerge when, once again, the wetland fills. Most impressive of all wetland inhabitants is the Estuarine, or Saltwater, Crocodile. It lives in northern coastal rivers and swamps, and may grow to more than six metres long, eating anything it can catch.

Above: *A wetland scene at Anbangbang Billabong in the Top End of the Northern Territory, where shallow swamps are flooded annually by the rainy season, known as The Wet.* **Inset:** *Wandering Whistling-Ducks.*

Top: *Estuarine Crocodiles in a companionable sprawl soak up the sunshine on a sandbank.* **Above:** *The eye of one of Nature's most formidable killers, the Estuarine Crocodile.*
Below, left: *The Barramundi is favoured prey with both human anglers and hunting crocodiles. Its life history takes it from the sea to fresh water.*
Below, right: *The Freshwater Crocodile grows to three metres long. It eats fish, frogs and birds, and is not dangerous to humans.*

Top: *Waterbirds at sunset on a typical northern Australian wetland.* **Above, left:** *A Comb-crested Jacana broods its eggs on its partly submerged nest of water plants.*
Above, right: *A male Darter in characteristic pose, drying its wings. Its gaping mouth shows why it can swallow quite large fish.* **Below, left:** *The Jabiru, or Black-necked Stork, hunts in grasslands bordering wetlands as well as along the water's edge.* **Below, right:** *A Great Egret patrols the shallows of a Kakadu wetland.*

Australia's wetlands, from the seasonal swamps of the north to the permanent coastal lakes of the south-east, from transient claypans in the Red Centre to sewage farms on the outskirts of major cities, are havens for waterbirds. They come in all sizes, shapes and colours, each species with its own niche in their shared watery habitat. Herons, egrets and spoonbills stalk through shallows or grasses, snapping up unwary frogs and crustaceans. Black-necked Storks, with their heavy-duty beaks, tackle larger prey, including sizeable snakes. Ducks paddle the shallows, up-ending to seize beakfuls of waterweed, while geese graze the grassland and Brolgas dig up tubers on swampy plains. The Comb-crested Jacana moves on long toes across lily leaves, dancing delicately forward as each foothold sinks below the surface. And, on snags and the branches of drowned trees, cormorants and snake-necked Darters hang out their wings to dry as they digest recently caught meals of shining-scaled fish.

Above: *These Black Swan cygnets will stay with their parents for up to six months. Black Swans may be seen anywhere in Australia where there is water, for they can fly long distances. They feed on waterweed and other wetland plants.*

Above, left: *White-lipped Tree-frogs, also known as Giant Tree-frogs, are the largest tree-frogs in the world. They grow up to 14 centimetres long and live in north-eastern Queensland.* **Above, right:** *The Green Tree-frog is a national icon.* **Below:** *Magnificent Tree-frogs live around water sources in the north-west of Western Australia.*

LIVING IN THE WETLANDS

Frogs are common in Australia's wetlands. Those that climb efficiently with the aid of adhesive pads on the ends of their fingers and toes spend the day in some refuge well above the ground. Others are burrowers, emerging from their shafts at night or during dull, rainy weather. All feed on any creature small enough to stuff into their cavernous mouths. In turn, they are hunted by lizards, snakes and birds. Less predatory waterside dwellers include the large, nectar- and fruit-eating bats known as flying-foxes, which spend the day in large groups called camps, and the nocturnal, leaf-eating ringtail possum, whose football-sized nest, lined with shredded bark or grass, is placed amongst foliage.

Above, left: *At dusk, this Spectacled Flying-fox will fly off in search of flowering or fruiting trees.* **Above, right:** *The Common Ringtail Possum eats foliage.*
Below, left: *Often found in groups, the Eastern Water Dragon lives near coastal creeks and waterways. It eats insects and fruit.*
Below, right: *The Red-bellied Black Snake eats frogs, reptiles and small mammals. It is venomous and its bite is potentially fatal to a human.*

Clockwise from above left: *An Eastern Pygmy-possum looking for nectar and insects on a banksia flower; Eastern Quolls are still found in Tasmanian heathland; Rainbow Bee-eaters eat the wasps and bees that come to heathland flowers.* **Below:** *A Scaly-breasted Lorikeet uses its brush-tipped tongue to plunder nectar from a grevillea flower.*

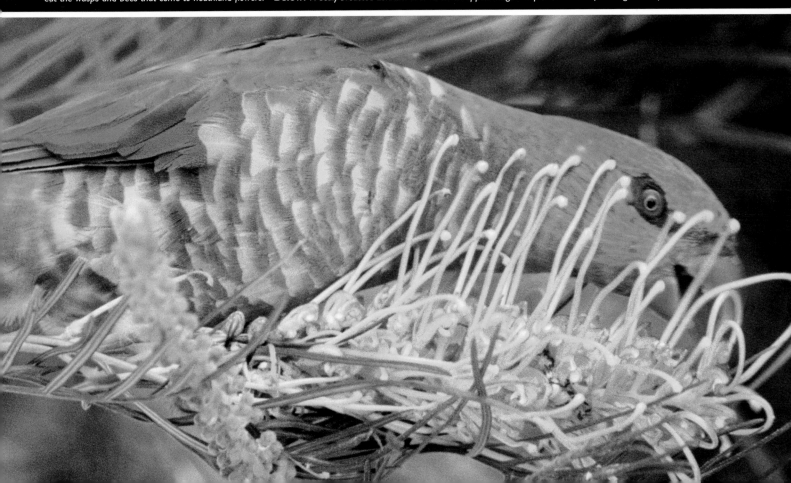

HEATHLANDS

The coastal heathlands that lie on the landward sides of dunes and beaches are often areas whose sandy soils are deficient in plant foods. Heathland plants have adapted to make the best of these conditions. Some species host nitrogen-fixing bacteria in nodules on their roots, while others interact with fungi that help them utilise what nutrients are available. They also have strategies for pollination and seed dispersal.

In springtime, heathland plants blossom abundantly. Birds such as honeyeaters and lorikeets, some small mammals and various insects have evolved in interaction with nectar-bearers such as banksias, eucalypts and bottlebrushes. They feed on protein-rich sweet fluid, then carry away golden grains of pollen that are transferred to the next flower visited. The wasps, bees, beetles and other insects attracted to the flowers provide a feast for insectivorous birds such as bee-eaters.

Above: *Southern coastal heathland in spring, when many species of wildflower blossom.*
Inset: *A male Eastern Spinebill probing a bottlebrush flower for nectar.*

Above: *A peaceful scene on the south-west section of Australia's long coastline.*
Inset: *A Little Penguin returns from a day's fishing to feed its chicks waiting in a nest dug into a sand dune.*

SEACOASTS AND OCEANS

The Australian mainland and Tasmania have a total coastline length of nearly 37 000 kilometres. The shoreline may be rocky, sandy or muddy, bordered by cliffs, dunes or mangrove swamps.

Animal life above the tide line reflects the nature of the life in the adjoining ocean, and there are a number of ways to appreciate its complexity and fascination. Strolling along any Australian beach brings rewards in observing seabirds and flotsam, crabs and other intertidal life. Investigating rock pools or coral reef flats opens up new worlds, while even richer experiences reward the snorkeller or scuba diver. The mangroves that border long stretches of the continent's northern coasts create remarkable habitats full of intriguing creatures that the human investigator, liberally anointed with insect repellent, should explore with caution. For the less adventurous, whale-watching from vantage points on the shore or from seagoing vessels is increasingly popular.

Above, left: *The White-bellied Sea-Eagle is found right around Australia's coastline. It takes fish from the surface with a spectacular swoop.*

Above, right: *The Silver Gull is common, particularly where anglers and picnickers give it hand-outs of food. It is a scavenger that feasts on the eggs of other seabirds.*

Below: *Australian Pelicans breed on inland wetlands as well as on the coast, but find their best hunting grounds in the ocean.*

Top: *A pair of Humpback Whales breach as they journey north to their breeding grounds along the Great Barrier Reef.*
Above, left: *The Whale Shark is a huge, harmless fish that feeds on plankton.* **Above, right:** *A female Australian Sea-lion and her pup.*
Below, left: *A Green Turtle reaches the sea again after laying her eggs in a pit dug in the beach.* **Below, right:** *Australian Fur-seal playing in a bed of Giant Kelp.*

Some of the earliest European settlements in Australia were made because of the profits to be gained from trading in body parts harvested from sea mammals. Humpback and Southern Right Whales, Australian Fur-seals and Sea-lions were slaughtered for oil, baleen "whalebone" and furry pelts until their numbers dwindled so much they were no longer worth hunting. It has taken many years for these creatures to increase again, and today observing them has become a national pastime.

Marine turtles are declining in numbers worldwide, and Australia's northern beaches contain some of the few places where they can still nest undisturbed. Females drag themselves above the high-tide mark, where, in laboriously dug holes, they deposit round, white eggs. They then return to the ocean, leaving their offspring to make their perilous way to the water when, months later, the eggs hatch.

Above: At a number of places on Australia's coastline, bottlenose dolphins come to shallow water to interact with humans. They live in groups called pods, and eat fish, squid and other marine life.

Above: *Two Oblique-banded Sweetlips shelter in a cave on the Great Barrier Reef.*
Inset: *A Vermilion Biscuit Star moves over a reef, using myriads of tiny tube feet on its underside.*

UNDERWATER LIFE

Past low-tide mark the seabed may consist of sand or mud, rocky reef or, where ocean temperatures rise to around 18°C or above, coral reef. The creatures that inhabit this waterworld may drift with the currents, or swim freely through the ocean, or live all their lives within one small area. They may be as huge as Manta Rays or as tiny as coral polyps; they may be placid plant-eaters or fierce predators. Some, such as the creatures that live in estuaries, may need to adapt constantly to drastic changes in water composition and temperature. Others may survive in places such as the lightless depths, where the water is always frigid, pressure is tremendous and any change means death.

The ocean's habitats are diverse and many creatures move freely between a number of them. Some of the strangest spend their immature stages being carried by the sea far from their birth places to their eventual settling places on soft bottoms, rocks, coral, jetties or the hulls of boats.

Top, left: *A pair of Reef Bannerfish.* **Top, right:** *A Yellow Damsel swims past gorgonian coral.*
Above, left: *A pair of Orange-fin Anemonefish with their home anemone.* **Above, right:** *The Lionfish can introduce venom into a wound made by its spiny fins.*
Below, left to right: *A pair of Pineapplefish; a Big-belly Seahorse anchors itself to a sponge; the Emperor Angelfish lives in deeper reef waters around northern Australia.*

Top, left: *Common Brushtail Possum and young.* **Top, right:** *A Rainbow Lorikeet feeds in a suburban garden.* **Above, left:** *A New Holland Honeyeater probes a garden flower.* **Above, right:** *The Northern Brown Bandicoot will venture into gardens and campsites across northern Australia.* **Below, left to right:** *The Pied Butcherbird has a melodious song; the Carpet Python makes its home in sheds, gardens and house ceilings; Australian Magpies live in groups, each of which defends a home territory.*

While some of Australia's wild creatures have become rarer, and a few have disappeared altogether, many manage to survive and even proliferate in suburban and urban habitats. Bandicoots dig their conical feeding holes in lawns where surrounding plant cover is thick enough to protect them from dogs; possums shriek away the night in gardens and ceilings; Tasmanian Devils enter suburbia in search of food, and, where bushland is near, Koalas may be seen perching sleepily in trees in outer-city parks. Reptiles such as the Bearded Dragon, Shingleback and Blue-tongue sun themselves in flower beds, while Carpet Pythons make their homes in garden sheds and Eastern Water Dragons roam near suburban watercourses. However, the prize for coexistence must go to the birds, from the black-and-white group that includes the butcherbirds, magpie and crows, to colonisers such as the parrots that crowd to flowering trees and feeders, the ibis and gulls that populate city parks, the plovers that nest on playing fields and traffic islands, and a host of others.

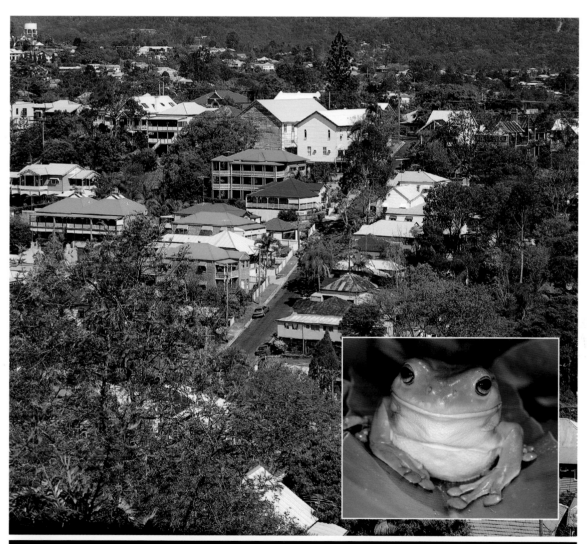

Above: *Wildlife establishes itself in many human settlements, especially if green corridors connect gardens and parks to bushland.* **Inset:** *The Green Tree-frog is common in northern gardens, toilets and gutters.*